AIR UNIVERSITY
AIR COMMAND AND STAFF COLLEGE

I0447417

A Game of Simon Says

Latin America's Left Turn and Its Effects on US Security

J. Lee Bennett
Lieutenant Commander, US Navy

Air Command and Staff College
Wright Flyer Paper No. 31

Air University Press
Maxwell Air Force Base, Alabama

May 2008

This Wright Flyer Paper and others in the series are available electronically at the Air University Research Web site http://research.maxwell.af.mil and the AU Press Web site http://aupress.maxwell.af.mil.

Disclaimer

Opinions, conclusions, and recommendations expressed or implied within are solely those of the author and do not necessarily represent the views of Air University, the United States Air Force, the Department of Defense, or any other US government agency. Cleared for public release: distribution unlimited.

Foreword

It is my great pleasure to present another of the *Wright Flyer Papers* series. In this series, the Air Command and Staff College (ACSC) recognizes and publishes our best student research projects from the prior academic year. The ACSC research program encourages our students to move beyond the school's core curriculum in their own professional development and in "advancing air and space power." The series title reflects our desire to perpetuate the pioneering spirit embodied in earlier generations of Airmen. Projects selected for publication combine solid research, innovative thought, and lucid presentation in exploring war at the operational level. With this broad perspective, the *Wright Flyer Papers* engage an eclectic range of doctrinal, technological, organizational, and operational questions. Some of these studies provide new solutions to familiar problems. Others encourage us to leave the familiar behind in pursuing new possibilities. By making these research studies available in the *Wright Flyer Papers*, ACSC hopes to encourage critical examination of the findings and to stimulate further research in these areas.

JIMMIE C. JACKSON, JR.
Brigadier General, USAF
Commandant

Abstract

A little over 200,000 votes in Mexico's 2006 presidential election determined whether or not the United States might soon share a border with a potentially communist country. A closer look reveals Mexico was nearly another domino in a rash of leftism that is sweeping through Latin America and the Caribbean (LAC). In fact, there are as many leftist countries in the LAC region today as there were in Eastern Europe at the height of the Cold War. This research will determine why leftism is on the rise and whether US national security is being threatened.

The causes are a combination of extreme inequality with regards to income per capita, an increased awareness among the populace as to its unequal situation, a poor display of US foreign policy, and an increase in education levels throughout the region. In short, Latin Americans are smarter, poorer, and angrier with the United States for its inattentiveness since the end of the Cold War.

The Bush administration's association of democracies with US national security is shown to be questionable. Hugo Chavez and Evo Morales were both democratically elected, and their associations with known terror organizations and rogue states decrease US security. In any case, most new leftist governments in Latin America are not true leftists. They are called leftist, but their external economic policies clearly resemble capitalism. Ironically, the effect on US national security depends upon its own future actions.

Based on these findings, three policy proposals are recommended. First, the United States needs to pioneer fairer trade agreements. Second, the United States needs to increase its foreign aid, with earmarks for economic investments. Third, the United States needs to work harder at being a good neighbor. These three steps should pull the region together and thereby increase the entire hemisphere's security.

Introduction

Roughly half of a single percentage point of the 41 million votes cast for president in Mexico's July 2006 elections determined whether or not the United States would share an immediate border with a potentially communist country.[1] That, to some, is a narrow escape when considering how much effort the United States has committed to ensuring the containment of communism, particularly in the Western Hemisphere, since the end of World War II. However, a closer look at the region south of the Rio Grande reveals Mexico was almost another domino in what can be described as the "second coming of Communism." Of the 22 most populated and sovereign countries that make up the Latin America and Caribbean (LAC) region,[2] nine now have a leftist executive at their government's head.[3] In fact, there are as many leftist countries in the LAC region today as there were in Eastern Europe at the height of the Cold War.[4] Venezuela's boisterous leader, Hugo Chavez, whose recent rhetoric has earned him front-page headlines all over the world, has joined forces with other like-minded LAC leaders, such as long-time US nemesis Fidel Castro, to form an anti-US coalition of the unwilling. This terminology is fitting because collectively they are reluctant to believe a long-promised US-led economic turnaround for the region will ever materialize and are unwilling to continue on the present course. From a US standpoint, simply throwing money at the problem has failed to create the desired effects of economic stability and a strengthened friendship with the rest of America. Over the previous 62 years, the United States has invested, on average, more than half a billion dollars per year into LAC countries,[5] a region that is perennially recognized as one of the poorest on earth.[6]

The United States has prided itself on being able to shield Latin American and Caribbean countries from foreign colonialism (Monroe Doctrine) and communism (Truman Doctrine). So why, after years of the United States' micromanagement of LAC internal politics—using every conceivable instrument of power known to the international community—has a recent rash of leftism swept through the region? Does this trend pose a significant threat to the national security of the United States? This paper argues that even though many administrations in these Latin American countries call themselves leftist, they are (for the most part) continuing to support free-market theory and free-trade agreements between states. However, a few countries are creating angst among the rest of the Americas due to their relationships with terrorist organizations and rogue states. Because of these factors, the effect of the leftist trend on the national security of the United States is yet to be determined. This paper concludes with some policy proposals that will help ease tensions between the United States and its southern neighbors and increase security throughout the region, but first we need to discuss what a leftist is exactly.

Left, Lefter, and Leftist

Ask any three Americans what the differences between leftism, communism, and socialism are, and you are likely to get a confused look in return. In fact, many scholars blur the nuances between these forms of government either purposely, in order to avoid the lengthy discussion regarding their differences, or accidentally, due to lack of proper research. However, it is essential to the purpose of this paper to accurately define and categorize socioeconomic descriptors in order to distinguish between the left and the right. Executive administrations are differentiated by their social constructs and economic theories; these two attributes will serve as the umbrellas under which each brand of government is filed.

A government's social construct identifies from whom it received its authority to govern and to whom the leadership is ultimately responsible. In an anarchy there is no legitimate government—each individual is guided by self-rule and is beholden to no one. Somalia of the early 1990s is the closest the world has come to witnessing total anarchy in modern times. Democracies, however, have executive branch leaders who are voted into office by an electorate drawn from the general population. A democratic or pluralistic society, in theory, allows each individual citizen an equal chance of becoming its head of state. Moreover, in a democracy, the populace has the right to change its leadership with each ensuing election if it so chooses. The United States is the most obvious example of this type of government, although there are many others in the world today. Conversely, an autocracy leads by decree, and its leader usually cannot be removed from power without force. This type of social construct is often called tyrannical, totalitarian, dictatorial, or monarchical and allows for the least amount of input from the general population regarding the country's direction. Some autocratic states may hold elections for show (e.g., Saddam Hussein's Iraq), but the results—much like a rigged carnival game—are predetermined and always favorable towards the incumbent. This falsely gives the outward appearance that the entrenched leaders are adored by the people they lead, thus solidifying the authority to govern.[7] If we imagine a pyramid structure, an anarchy would be its base (little or no vertical rise because no person has official authority over another), a democracy would be the centerpiece (gaining power from the electorate to boost freely elected officials who can eventually be brought back down), and an autocracy would be the apex (power concentrated in a few or a single person). Although these types of governments describe sources of power, they should not be automatically correlated with those on the left or right of the political spectrum based upon their economic disposition.

A government's established economic theory describes its relative position on a linear scale. On the right side of this scale is a purely capitalistic society where the state has no say whatsoever regarding what products the country will make and sell. The government and its economy are independent from one another but are also dependent upon the other's existence for survival. It is important to note that there are no purely capitalistic societies in existence in today's world. Even the United States' public exhibition of free-market capitalism is not without some governmental intervention. The US Postal Service is solely a state-run organization while others, such as Amtrak—the nation's only passenger rail service—are highly subsidized by the federal government and are, hence, subject to its oversight. On the opposite (left) side of this scale is the economy that is completely state-owned and operated. The government dictates who, what, how, when, and to what extent items will be made and sold. These types of economies are often practiced in an attempt to equally distribute all of a country's resources among its citizens. Communism, collectivism,

Leninism, Marxism, and socialism are some of the more familiar variants of leftism.[8] Most importantly, a country's economic theory and social construct are mutually exclusive descriptors, and any correlation between the two should never be implied.

Many people automatically (and incorrectly) assume a relationship between a government's social construct and economic theory. For example, oftentimes a democracy (a freely elected government) will be associated with capitalism (a free-market economy). Likewise, autocracies are often linked with leftism. These types of governments, while traditionally conjoined, are not always together. For example, Hong Kong, although a city and not a state, is a prime example of how an autocratic capitalist government could exist in modern times. Likewise, democratic socialism is very popular in Europe. The United Kingdom's Labour Party is among the largest in existence today, and Sweden can be considered a socialist state with a democratically elected government. Similarly, many LAC countries are democratically electing governments with leftist economic policies, the reasons for which are examined in the next few sections.

"Who Lost Latin America?"

An examination of this region's political history reveals that many countries have broken free from the chains of colonialism only to have their freedom frequently stymied by autocratic or military rule. Of the 22 LAC countries researched for this paper, most have been ruled by a dictator or military junta (or both) at least once since declaring their "independence"; and for some, a coup d'état seems to be the normal method of transitioning from one executive administration to another.[9] For example, Panama's president, Arnulfo Arias Madrid, was democratically elected on three separate occasions (1940, 1949, and 1968) but never served a full term in office because he was deposed by his military each time.[10] Some could argue the current leftist trend is simply the political pendulum swinging back and forth due to the current feelings of the electorate—a temporary motion consistent within most democracies and one that will eventually return to the right. However, the region's historically unstable democracies, combined with the

4

inability to differentiate between the economic practices of each individual LAC administration, makes this theory of a left-right cyclical pattern difficult to prove or disprove. Due to time and length limitations, this paper does not include data in an attempt to demonstrate the validity of this type of model. Moreover, it has recently become commonly accepted among academics and news media that there is, in fact, a wave of leftism currently sweeping through the LAC region. As one *New York Times* author declared, "Since a bombastic army colonel, Hugo Chavez, won office in Venezuela in 1998, three-quarters of South America has shifted to the left."[11] This paper proceeds under that assumption, accepting the much ballyhooed trend as fact while answering the question, who lost Latin America?[12]

Such a movement towards leftism may appear frightening to some ultraconservative capitalists, but in order to determine how this swing will truly affect US national security, we must first understand why it is happening. There are as many theories accounting for why LAC countries are leaning leftward as there are ethnic groups living within the region. However, like the descriptors of a national government, most of these theories can be codified into two categories: economic and social. Economically, history has shown us how extreme inequality between a few rich elitists and the majority poor class can lead to a situation where a revolutionary shift to a polar opposite style of government may result.[13] In addition, US foreign policy decisions, such as reducing the amount of foreign aid to the region, may have contributed to the turn of public opinion against the US government and its policies towards their suddenly forgotten friends to the south—thus "pushing" LAC voters to find a more appealing candidate on the opposite side of the political spectrum. Socially, increased education levels may lead to a more intelligent and informed electorate that desires to change its station in life through voting. Marta Lagos, head of the Chile-based polling organization Latinobarómetro (which surveys social and political attitudes in 18 Latin American countries), agreed in an interview with *Miami Herald* columnist Andres Oppenheimer, saying that "Latin Americans with the highest levels of education tend to have the most negative views of the United States."[14] More likely, however, it is a combination of these economic and social factors that is setting the Latin American stage for silver-tongued populist candidates who are skilled in the art of politics and can assemble a following sizable enough to sweep them into office. Specifically, these leftist, populist candidates are drawing attention to the degree of poverty within their countries, the reason for which will be discussed next.

"There's One for You, Nineteen for Me"

To declare that the LAC region is poor is misleading—it has wealth and growth, just not for the majority of its people. A quick comparison of gross domestic product (GDP) per capita (adjusted for purchasing power parity [PPP]) by global region shows LAC countries are wedged securely between the most economically advanced nations and the world's poorest nations. The LAC's 2004 figure of $7,964 per person is less than the per capita GDP-PPP of people who reside in the countries belonging to the Organization for Economic Cooperation and Development ($27,571) and Central and Eastern Europe ($8,802).[15] However, this figure is higher than that which is earned in a single year by the nearly four billion people who live elsewhere around the world and is more than four times the current level found in sub-Saharan Africa ($1,946).[16] Moreover, the LAC's GDP-PPP per capita growth rate from the end of the Cold War until 2004 has been a respectable 1.1 percent, only slightly less than the world average of 1.4 percent during that same time frame.[17]

Unfortunately, per capita figures are deceptive in that they do not tell the complete story regarding distribution of wealth within the area measured. To show this, we must review the region's "Gini coefficient." A Gini coefficient, named for Italian statistician Corrado Gini, provides a quick reference as to how evenly the wealth of a country or region is distributed. A coefficient of 1.0 indicates perfect inequality (all the money is possessed by a single person), and a coefficient of 0.0 indicates perfect equality (every citizen possesses the same amount of wealth). It is with this economic indicator that we find our proverbial smoking gun of poverty within the LAC context. As one academic demonstrated, "Latin America is the most inequitable region worldwide, where no one single country reaches even the median level of the Gini of Sub Saharan Africa."[18] Moreover, the LAC region has consistently had household per-capita- income Gini coefficients greater than 0.50 as far back as these figures have been recorded, while other regions of the world have never had an average break the 0.50 level in any documented year.[19] In comparison, most developed countries have a Gini coefficient in the 0.30 to 0.40 range. To provide context to these figures, note that "the richest tenth of the people in the [LAC] region earn 48 percent of total income, the poorest tenth earn only 1.6 percent."[20] This equates to a 30-to-1 ratio—a distribution more lopsided than even the lyrics from the 1966 Beatles' song "Taxman" envisioned. Alvaro Hurtado of the International Labour Organization states that the problem is only getting worse because "the region has shown the most regressive distribution of income of the world throughout the twentieth century."[21]

Being poor is bad enough, but being poor and knowing that your neighbor has more money than he knows what to do with can make people jealous and angry and generate the urge to "correct" the situation. As a 2001 Latinobarómetro poll illustrates, almost 90 percent of LAC citizens think the income distribution in their country is either unfair or very unfair.[22] According to Dr. Anthony Lott, this awareness of the inequalities that exist within their countries creates unrest in a way that poverty does not. He states that if all of a country's citizens were poverty stricken (with a Gini coefficient of 0.0), they would not know what benefits increased wealth could bring them and, therefore, would not be upset by its absence. However, he continues, community members that can visualize their poverty through a comparison with the wealthiest 10 percent of their population will be much more likely to take action in an attempt to alleviate their unnecessary suffering.[23] Such a scenario could certainly lead to a shift in the political landscape of a region to a party that is more traditionally associated with an equal-distribution-of-wealth platform (i.e., leftism). As Enrique ter Horst of the *International Herald Tribune* states, "The poor have also discovered the power of the vote, and developed a keen attachment to free elections."[24] To the LAC electorate, changing to a leftist government—rightly or wrongly—is *menos mal* (less bad) when compared to the status quo.

In addition to searching for new leadership to correct the region's wealth inequality, poverty-stricken LAC citizens are looking for alternate sources of income. Unfortunately for them, however, their once abundant supply of inward-bound foreign aid has significantly decreased as well.

Heavy-Handed Diplomacy

If Latin America's unequal wealth distribution has provided the force necessary to create kinetic energy for change within the populace, then the United States' foreign policy towards the region, specifically the conscious decision to lessen its amount of aid, has established direction. The resultant vector, however, is away from Latin America's friendship with the United States and towards a leftist-led subregional unity. According to the US Agency for International Development's (USAID) "Greenbook," between the end of World War II and the breakup of the Soviet Bloc, the United States gave its fellow Americans more than $26 billion in order to offset pro-leftist funds from the Soviet Union and to protect US interests in the region.[25] At its peak, the United States gave over $1.9 billion to Latin American countries in 1990 in order to ensure free-market democracies stayed in power, the eighth consecutive year of providing $1 billion or more. However, Big Brother's aid dropped significantly following the fall of communism in Europe to a mere $695 million in 1996.[26] Once the financial faucet was turned off from the left, it was no longer in the United States' self-interest to supply the LAC countries with counterbalancing funds, especially in an era of competing priorities and limited financial resources.

Even worse for future relations, the United States is using its checkbook to coerce LAC leadership into falling in line with its own interests. Congress passed the American Servicemembers' Protection Act in 2002 wherein it declared no US military personnel or government employee will stand trial in the International Criminal Court (ICC) for crimes delineated in the Rome Statute of the same year. "The law cuts off . . . aid to countries that are signatories" of the statute "unless the country has signed a so-called 'Article 98' agreement, pledging not to seek prosecution of U.S. citizens in the ICC."[27] To date, "twelve Latin American countries have bucked pressure from the Bush Administration" to sign the immunity agreement,[28] and "as a result, Washington has cut the funding it supplies to those nations."[29] Latin American nations have responded as one might expect to the threat of cuts in aid. Ecuadorian president Alfredo Palacio declared, "Absolutely no one is going to make me cower." Costa Rican foreign minister Roberto Tovar called the immunity proposals "offensive" and added that "one can be poor, but dignified."[30]

As another example of coercive tactics, US officials reportedly threatened to "impose economic sanctions and other punitive measures if [Daniel] Ortega was reelected" for another term as president of Nicaragua.[31] Nicaraguans failed to heed this warning and elected Ortega to the presidency in November 2006, possibly as a direct reaction against US pressures. These examples of US foreign policy with respect to Latin America and the Caribbean are only some of the most egregious ones in a long history of heavy-handedness. Without recounting history, let it suffice to say the United States has been meddling in LAC internal politics since the Monroe Doctrine was first established, and the peoples of the region are starting to get annoyed by the constant interference coming from their bullying neighbor to the north. Columnist Niall Ferguson summed up the relationship very succinctly when he wrote, "The only Central American state that hasn't found itself on the receiving end of at least one US military intervention is Costa Rica."[32]

The United States' lack of concern for anything other than its own self-interests has infuriated some Latin Americans, causing them to have a less than favorable opinion of their former close ally and financial supporter. A December 2004 BBC/Globescan/Program on International Policy Attitudes poll shows most citizens from the four LAC countries who participated in the survey believe the United States has a "mostly negative influence in the world" and view Pres. George W. Bush's reelection as "negative for peace and security in the world."[33] Similarly, as a 2006 Latinobarómetro poll reveals, "three out of every five Latin Americans distrust the United States."[34] However, as previously demonstrated with GDP-PPP per capita, dissecting the LAC population into the elites and general population exposes a huge division between their opinions. A September 2005 *Miami Herald/*

University of Miami Business School/Zogby International poll shows that "Latin America's elites are more critical of the United States, and tend to describe themselves as more left of center than the rest of the population."[35] This survey of government officials, journalists, business executives, and academics from six LAC countries (Argentina, Brazil, Chile, Colombia, Mexico, and Venezuela) shows "only one in four members of the Latin American elites held a favorable view of Bush."[36] A 2004 Latinobarómetro poll of the LAC's general population "found that a majority picked the United States" when "asked to name their country's 'best friend in the world,' " compared to only 12 percent of elites who were asked a similar question in the 2005 Zogby poll.[37] This juxtaposition of data leads the interpreter to conclude that the higher-educated elitists of LAC countries "tend to have the most negative views of the United States" while, as Marta Lagos explains, those with "the lowest education levels still believe in the American dream."[38] That being the case, the next obvious question needing to be studied is whether education levels in the region are rising or falling.

Knowledge Is Power

Since 1990, education measures of merit for Latin America and the Caribbean as a whole have steadily improved across the board. The region's level of education is definitely improving, and in some areas the increases are keeping pace with those of the most advanced countries. The average schooling years of LAC countries from 1990 to 2000 increased from 5.2 to 5.9. This increase of 0.7 years is exactly the same as the increase witnessed in economically advanced countries during the same period. In fact, LAC average years of schooling have increased every decade since 1960. Of the 22 countries examined for this research, 20 showed increases in their average schooling years from 1990 to 2000, with Peru being the most improved (5.9 years in 1990 to 7.3 years in 2000).[39] Similar progress is seen in the region's literacy rates. Adult literacy rates (ages 15 and older) increased in 16 of the 17 countries where data was available, with Honduras showing the most improvement (68.1 percent in 1990 to 80 percent in 2004) and Jamaica being the only regression (82.2 percent in 1990 to 79.9 percent in 2004).[40] Likewise, youth literacy rates increased in all 16 countries where data was available, with Nicaragua leading the pack (68.2 percent in 1990 to 86.2 percent in 2004).[41]

However, if a government's expenditure percentage on education is a lead indicator for future education levels, the region may be heading into trouble. When education disbursements are measured as a percentage of total government expenditures, only five out of 10 countries showed an increase between 1991 and 2004. Percentages in Chile, Cuba, El Salvador, Nicaragua, and Paraguay went up while those in Costa Rica, Colombia, Jamaica, Panama, and Uruguay went down (no data was available for the remaining 12 countries). As a percentage of the GDP, the figures are only slightly better. Education disbursements between 1991 and 2004 went up for 11 of the 14 countries where data was available.[42]

As a region, LAC citizens are getting better educated (for now). Armed with this increased knowledge, acutely aware of their unequal financial situation, and tired of playing the subservient role to the United States' perceived self-centered demands, Latin Americans are turning to new leaders to help them emerge from their currently deplorable situation. These populists, with their fresh ideas and sometimes strong anti-US rhetoric, are taking advantage of the situation and driving their countries leftward at a potentially alarming rate. The question of what this trend means for US national security should now be the primary concern for anyone who is watching with interest as the dominoes fall in Latin America.

"La Roma Americana"

In the cover letter for the 2006 *National Security Strategy of the United States of America*, President Bush wrote, "Our national security is founded upon two pillars." Those pillars are then listed as "promoting freedom, justice and dignity" and "leading a growing community of democracies." His justification for linking world democracies to US national security is that "free governments do not . . . attack each other."[43] A similar statement exists in the introduction section to the February 2003 *National Strategy for Combating Terrorism*, wherein President Bush explains that one of the keys to defeating terrorism is to "integrate nations and peoples into the mutually beneficial democratic relationships that protect against the forces of disorder and violence."[44] It is clear from these documents that the Bush administration is linking democratic societies to world peace in general and US national security specifically. However, the wave of leftism that we are currently witnessing in the LAC region is the *result* of democracy.[45] An electorate freely choosing to vote anyone into office, even a leftist, is demonstrating democracy in action. As Ferguson explains, "Democracy doesn't always produce liberal governments."[46] As a result, the United States' national security can be described by some as being more tenuous today than it was before the current trend began.

The Cuban constitution of 1976 called for the "integration of Latin America and Caribbean nations" against, among other things, "imperialism"—or as Cuban Independence hero José Martí quipped, "la Roma Americana."[47] Now, over 30 years later, we are witnessing such a union in the Bolivarian Alternative for the Americas, which was "conceived as a much larger process of alternative integration for Latin America and the Caribbean,"[48] and the Sao Paulo Forum, which is described as "a Castro-inspired international group of rogue states and terrorist groups."[49] Although democratic, this "alternative integration" may be translating into a less secure environment for the United States through a larger anti-US coalition in Latin America that has increased connections with international terrorist organizations, such as Hezbollah, and more formal relations with countries that are adversarial to the United States, like Iran.

Hezbollah, the self-proclaimed "Party of God," is an organization that is well known throughout the world for its terrorist intent towards the state of Israel and its Western allies, but Hezbollah's global connections, specifically those in the LAC region, may be lesser known. "Its chief sponsor is the Islamic Republic of Iran, which provides major financial support as well as weapons and paramilitary training. Syria . . . also lends substantial support."[50] Venezuela can be added to that list. Hezbollah has "been using Venezuela—mostly Margarita Island and Maracaibo . . . to focus on illicit financial dealings and counterfeiting."[51] "After Chavez visited Lebanon last summer, a Hezbollah official told an

Indian newspaper, 'Mr. Chavez is closer to us than any other Arab leader'"—but Hezbollah is not the only terror group Venezuela is engaged with these days.[52] According to Gen James Hill, former head of the US Southern Command, Margarita Island (Venezuela) is also a known location for other terrorist support cells, such as Hamas and Islamiyya al Gammat.[53] Another former head of US Southern Command, Gen Gary Speer, testified before the Senate Armed Services Committee in March 2002 that he was "very concerned about President Chavez [since] the FARC [Fuerzas Armadas Revolucionarias de Colombia or Revolutionary Armed Forces of Colombia] operates at will across the border into Venezuela."[54] The FARC is a guerrilla terrorist organization that protects drug cartels and whose ultimate goal is to overthrow Colombia's democratically elected pro-US government and replace it with its own Marxist-style (leftist) government.[55]

In addition to providing safe refuge, the Venezuelan government has supplied thousands of national identification cards, called *cedulas*, "to people from Cuba, Colombia, and Middle Eastern 'countries of interest' like Syria, Egypt, Pakistan and Lebanon that host foreign terrorist organizations."[56] These *cedulas* can be used to obtain Venezuelan passports, which can then be used to obtain travel visas to other countries and thereby possibly avoid red flags during immigration checks.[57] In February 2003, Hasil Mohamad Rahaman, who carried an authentic Venezuelan passport, was arrested at London's Gatwick Airport because he "was caught carrying a live hand grenade in his carry-on bag shortly after arriving from Caracas. Security experts believe he intended to detonate it aboard the plane or at the airport."[58]

Venezuela, unfortunately, is just the tip of the proverbial iceberg when it comes to harboring members of international terror organizations in Latin America. "Hezbollah has long used parts of South America as a training ground, in particular the tri-border area where Brazil, Argentina, and Paraguay meet."[59] The tri-border region is a near lawless part of the world, "which according to U.S. and Argentine officials has an Arab population of more than 20,000."[60] The sheer numbers of reported relations between LAC countries and terrorist groups is unsettling and raises the level of concern for the overall national security of the United States.

Moreover, the overt agreements between LAC countries and states that are seen as rivals with the United States on the world stage add another layer of apprehension.

Known by the Company You Keep

Most people would not find it surprising to hear that Cuba's Castro "maintains close ties with many terror groups and rogue states such as Iran and North Korea."[61] However, what might be shocking are the connections between the new Latin American leftists and countries that are seen as adversaries to the United States. "In 2001, Chavez paid state visits to and signed 'cooperation agreements' with Libya, Iraq and Iran" and "condemned America's Afghanistan campaign as 'fighting terrorism with terrorism.'"[62] These events were in conjunction with his providing "$1 million to al-Qaida soon after the Sept. 11 attacks."[63] During a showdown with the United States over making progress in the area of nuclear power, Iranian president Mahmoud Ahmadinejad completed "a whirlwind series of meetings with Latin America's newly inaugurated leftist leaders," paying visits to the leaders of Venezuela, Nicaragua, Ecuador, and Bolivia. During this tour, the Iranian leader pledged "deeper ties" and promised "to spend billions of dollars financing projects in other countries to combat global influence of their common enemy, the United States."[64] Attempting to drive a wedge between the United States and the rest of the Americas, Ahmadinejad said, "The imperialists don't like us to help you progress and develop. They don't like us to get rid of poverty and unite people."[65] The Iranian president appears to be utilizing the media to underscore his discontent with US foreign policies, much like we are currently witnessing in the LAC region.

While Iran's partnerships in the LAC region seem to have been designed to gain international attention, China has attempted to maintain a low profile while building a supportive coalition based on trade. Noticeably, however, "more and more Latin American countries are taking exception with Washington's economic prescriptions and those of the International Monetary Fund. Some are strengthening ties with China, which is investing heavily in the region."[66] In 2004 Chinese president Hu Jintao paid state visits to

Argentina, Brazil, Chile, and Cuba "where he signed 16 bilateral trade agreements."[67] Chinese trade has recently expanded in almost every LAC country.[68] "Economic necessities have convinced many Latin American and Caribbean countries that trade with China provides a good counterbalance to trade asymmetry with the United States."[69]

Arguably, simple trade agreements between the region and China is nothing for the United States to be worried about, but other joint projects (such as military research and development) and the building of strong relationships that threaten the current balance of power at the United Nations (UN) can be reason for concern. Alejandro Kenny observes that Brazil and China "work closely in the aerospace arena. They jointly developed and launched two research satellites and plan to launch another two by 2008." Moreover, "Chinese military delegations have visited Latin America to gain experience in a number of areas." Kenny adds that the LAC region and China have had several military-related exchanges recently, including visits by ministers of defense and other high-ranking military officials, a three-month military doctrine and national defense course held in Beijing, and a seminar in China for high-level military officers from Latin America regarding the future between China and the region. Additionally, aside from the military dealings, "China's relations with Latin America support other Chinese goals, such as the diplomatic isolation of Taiwan," and "the significant Latin American voting bloc in the U.N. also stirs Chinese interest."[70] A LAC region sympathetic to the People's Republic of China (PRC) argument that Taiwan is part of mainland China could be detrimental to the United States should the need arise to garner support at the UN for defense of the island. In addition to relationships external to the region, internal controversies between governments could destabilize the current level of peace and lead to inter-American fighting.

Regional Destabilization

Although Hugo Chavez is dishing out millions of barrels of oil at reduced cost and gobbling up the debt of fellow regional leftists (Argentina and Ecuador), he is not as well liked outside Venezuela and Cuba as one might be led to believe.[71] Both his actions and his words are beginning to wear thin the patience of Americans on both sides of the Rio Grande. Secretary of State Condoleezza Rice called Venezuela's Chavez a "destabilizing force" within the Latin American region.[72] Former US intelligence chief, now deputy secretary of state, John Negroponte testified before the Senate Foreign Relations Committee that he thinks Chavez's "behavior is threatening to democracies in the region."[73] Former secretary of defense Donald Rumsfeld compared Chavez to "the original National Socialist, Adolf Hitler."[74] Significantly, outside the US government the criticisms are similarly harsh, and often from fellow leftists. Peru's president, Alan Garcia, said Chavez "speaks under the influence of 'too much rum.' "[75] Juan Forero writes in the *New York Times* that this followed the decision of Peru's previous president, Alejandro Toledo, to recall his country's ambassador to Venezuela due to "flagrant interference" in Peru's internal affairs. Former Mexican foreign minister Jorge Castañeda agrees, saying Chavez "goes around shooting from the hip and shooting his mouth off, and that causes tensions." Peruvian, Mexican, Nicaraguan, and Brazilian officials "have expressed rising impatience at what they see as Mr. Chavez's meddling and grandstanding, often at their expense," the article continues. Moreover, Riordan Roett, the director of Latin American studies at Johns Hopkins University's School of Advanced International Studies, believes Chavez "is beginning to overreach, wanting to be involved in everything." Brazil's foreign minister, Celso Amorim, testified before his nation's senators that Pres. Lula da Silva "had admonished the Venezuelan leader in a private phone call" after being publicly humiliated, Forero adds.[76]

It appears Chavez's regional popularity may be suffering due to the same reasons the United States' has in the past—interfering in a sovereign state's internal affairs tends to make people not like you. These intergovernmental disagreements may be translating into a less stable Latin America. However, some still tolerate Chavez because he "is sitting on top of 6.5% of the world's proven oil reserves" and is willing to share the profits no matter the economic cost to his own country—but even those "friendships" may last only as long as oil prices are high.[77]

Chavez's protégé, Bolivia's leftist president Evo Morales, is probably Chavez's closest ally behind Castro, but even Morales is beginning to experience chaffing with fellow leftists over his trade and industry decisions, which may lead to an economic downturn for numerous countries in the region. Morales won the presidency campaigning on the promise to legalize the cultivation of coca (the prime ingredient required for making cocaine) and to take state control over the oil and natural gas industry. "Any and all of these steps," write *New York Times* reporters Juan Forero and Larry Rohter, "could unsettle Washington and the region." They note that among the many countries watching this development with concern is Brazil since "about half the natural gas consumed in Brazil comes from Bolivia," where a state-run oil and gas industry will most assuredly cause export prices to rise. Brazil also "worries about rising drug and crime problems in its urban slums if Bolivia's coca crop is not controlled."[78] Ferero and Rohter report that Argentina had a long-standing deal with Bolivian governments to receive "gas at below market prices," but Morales said recently that he "planned to end that arrangement."[79]

Like Chavez, Morales does not seem to care whom he offends with his words. The Bolivian president recently called President Bush a "terrorist" and said the United States "wants to convert Chile into the Israel of Latin America"—a statement that brought ire from all three countries simultaneously.[80] A former llama herder and the country's first indigenous leader, Morales believes "the state needs to be the central actor to plan economic development."[81] Unfortunately for Bolivians and their neighbors, President Morales has experience with neither economics nor diplomacy—two things that are essential for good economic planning. If there is any silver lining to this leftist cloud hanging over Latin America, it lies in the fact that most of the region's leftists are not practicing true leftism—at least in global economic terms.

Leftist in Name Only

Besides Latin America's "Axis of Evil" (Cuba, Venezuela, and Bolivia), most of the region's governments appear to be "leftist in name only" (LINO) opportunists who campaigned as leftists in order to garner support and votes. In the United States they would be called "Blue Dog Democrats," but in their home countries they are called populists, democratic socialists, or just plain leftists. Latin Americans, despite their opinions of President Bush and the United States, understand what is needed to get their countries out of poverty. According to a Latinobarómetro survey, "63 percent of the citizens in the region agreed that the market economy was the only means to develop their countries." Furthermore, two conservative administrations, Colombia and Mexico, and two leftist administrations, Chile and Brazil, have all produced "governments that will persist on their current path of fiscal responsibility and continued integration into the global economy."[82] Chilean socialist Michelle Bachelet has "repeatedly emphasized her commitment to following and expanding the pro-market, free-trade economic model pursued by the past three governments," while Brazilian president da Silva "has also proven to be a market champion."[83] Brazil and Uruguay "practice the kind of fiscal restraints accepted by Wall Street."[84] The "Brazilian Model," as described by one journalist, "is characterized by . . . increasing flows of domestic and foreign investment that create well-paying jobs and more exports."[85] Even Nicaragua's leftist president Ortega, a living icon of US intervention into LAC internal affairs, is believed to be pro-market these days. *Newsweek*'s Joseph Contreras writes that Ortega has "promised to respect private property" and to "keep inflation in check." Furthermore, a senior policy analyst for the Heritage Foundation, a conservative Washington-based think tank, agrees that the members of Ortega's party are "much more centrist and recognize that markets and democracy have their place."[86]

As with most of these LINO governments, "Peru has followed the road of political openness and free market reforms for its own good and not to please Washington."[87] However, the executive director of Bolivia's Democracy Center, Jim Schultz, believes "there's a common thread that runs through [these new leftist governments] to a certain degree, and that thread is a popular challenge to the market fundamentalism of the Washington Consensus."[88] These governments are making a clear and striking distinction between Washington's view of free trade and that which is required to pump life back into Latin American economies. Long gone are the days when Washington could insist on LAC countries signing a trade agreement that showed favoritism to US products. Latin Americans have figured out they can trade with each other or with other economies that are growing increasingly large (e.g., China and India). When the US and USSR foreign-aid spigots ran dry, LAC countries scrambled to find other means of economic flow, and they found it in foreign trade. Now, the United States is left trying to figure out exactly how to win back the trust of its fellow Americans.

Conclusions and Policy Proposals

This paper has demonstrated that Latin Americans are increasingly more educated and acutely aware of their extreme inequality. In addition, the region's citizens have taken a stance against the arm-twisting diplomatic tactics used by the United States. Americans south of the Rio Grande want equality, both monetary and social, and they are desperate to find the next Simón Bolivar—a liberator who can lead them to this ultimate goal.

The effect of this leftward trend on the national security of the United States is more complicated and requires a much more detailed and lengthy analysis. Venezuela's Chavez and Bolivia's Morales were each democratically elected but have since harbored terror organizations, cultivated relations with US adversaries, and created tensions with their neighboring countries. From that perspective, the national security of the United States is threatened, and it calls into question President Bush's assertion that democracies increase world peace and enhance US national security. However, it is promising to note that six of the nine leftist governments in Latin America practice capitalist-like economic policies. These LINO governments are creating tighter bonds among many countries in the Western Hemisphere. In spite of Chavez's rhetoric, even "Venezuela's own trade with the United States is booming like never before."[89] When considering Thomas Friedman's "Golden Arches theory of conflict prevention," the region as a whole may actually be more secure than it was before the Bolivarian Revolution began. His theory provides the astute realization that "no two countries that both had McDonald's had fought a war against each other since each got its McDonald's."[90] The reason is because globalization, the practice that creates interconnected economies, discourages war due to the effect it has on the global economy and, thus, the attacking country's own economy.[91] As a potential threat of nuclear exchange during the Cold War brought about the theory of a mutually assured destruction (if either side launched a nuclear strike, both sides would be destroyed), war in the era of globalization brings us to a mutually assured economic destruction (if any globalized country attacks another globalized country, both will suffer economically).

Since the quantification of US national security is beyond the scope of this paper, the impact of these trends is left to be determined by future research. Instead, suffice it to say the national security of the United States will be dramatically affected by its future actions, including in its own hemisphere, and it must therefore consider carefully the implications of its policies. There are three such actions which, if put into practice, should tip the scale in favor of a more peaceful and economically profitable hemisphere.

The United States is at least partially responsible for the current situation in Latin America and the Caribbean through its inattention to the needs of its neighbors. Fortunately, it is not too late to correct these conditions. The steps the United States needs to take in order to get back into good graces with its neighbors south of the Rio Grande are to pioneer better (more fair) trade agreements, attach more appropriate stipulations to foreign aid, and work harder at creating better diplomatic relations. These actions, in conjunction with Latin America's continuing commitment to equalizing the region's distribution of wealth, will get Latin America back on track to becoming more economically sound and solidify the region's democratic foundation.

There are numerous free-trade agreements either already in effect or in the planning stages. The North American Free Trade Agreement (NAFTA), the Central American Free Trade Agreement (CAFTA), and the numerous smaller ones are often chastised by some extreme leftists (i.e., Chavez et al.) as having a favorable slant towards the imperialistic United States. Subsidies, although a seemingly trifling act of nationalism to most US citizens, impact the sale of Latin

American and Caribbean goods more significantly, with specificity towards LAC's poorest workers—its farmers. Redrawing free-trade agreements to include verbiage seeking to eliminate all subsidies will create a more level playing field for Latin American farmers and assist in increasing their wealth. However, given the current state of affairs, even a level playing field may not be enough to jump-start the economic turnaround required in the poorest sectors of Latin America's economy. Quite possibly what will be required is an agreement that grants a temporary lopsided trade balance in favor of the poorer countries—similar to parts of the Marshall Plan of 1947. For example, a five-year unbalanced trade agreement will give the smaller, poorer markets in LAC countries the advantage they need to get themselves caught up to the rest of the world with respect to infrastructures associated with large-scale economic operations. This initial five-year plan should then be followed by a level field for all participants that will carry on until the end of the signed agreement (20 years maximum). At the conclusion of this 20-year cycle, the countries can then assess the effectiveness of their trade agreement and make adjustments necessary for future ones.

Complementary to the new trade agreement, the United States needs to restart its foreign aid to the Latin American region but with stipulations that are more appropriate than those used in the past. Instead of associating monetary assistance with votes for pro-US political parties, these moneys should be earmarked for items that will directly affect economic stimulation. For example, foreign aid given to a LAC country that will be used for building better roads, bridges, seaports or airports, communications, and rail systems will pay dividends in two ways. First, it will put people to work in the construction of their new infrastructure. Second, when completed, these items will increase business productivity and allow those citizens who are currently isolated miles away from their country's closest means of exportation to link up with the world economy. This is much like Pres. Franklin Roosevelt's New Deal plan, which was a major contributor to the United States' emergence from the depression years. The ultimate goal is to perpetuate growth in the region—better infrastructure leads to economic development, which leads to more jobs being created, which leads to the need for more and better infrastructures. Additionally, part of that aid can be used to assist Latin Americans in getting plugged into the World Wide Web where LAC's entrepreneurs can more easily compete for contracts they are currently excluded from due to limitations in connectivity.

Lastly, but probably the most important piece to this diplomatic puzzle, the United States needs to work harder at being a good neighbor. Hurricane Stan slammed Central America in October 2005 during that region's rainy season. Mudslides and severe flooding brought by the hurricane combined with the region's recent earthquakes and volcanic activity to kill nearly 1,000 and displace over one million. Karen Hughes, undersecretary of state for public diplomacy, visited Guatemala, the country hardest hit, shortly afterwards "virtually empty-handed," according to Lisa Haugaard in *Tarnished Image*. The Bush administration "did not choose to provide a new, substantial aid package" but decided instead to redirect existing aid. This response "stood in considerable contrast to the U.S. response to Hurricane Mitch [in 1998] . . . (when aid reached $750 million) and did not escape notice in the Central American press," says Haugaard. At a press conference during her visit to Guatemala, Hughes denied temporary protected status to Guatemalans living in the United States, which would have allowed them to send "$2 billion in annual remittances to their families . . . thus contributing to the relief effort," nor did she announce any reconstruction aid package. All this took place on the heels of Hurricane Katrina when "many Latin American nations rushed to offer something, even if only symbolic, to their powerful neighbor."[92] Certainly an opportunity to give the impression of friendship was lost with this display of callousness. Like familiarity, insensitivity breeds contempt. With diplomacy like this, Oppenheimer surmises that "you don't have to be a genius to figure out why Washington is losing influence in Latin America."[93]

Instead of building metaphorical bridges, the United States is spending billions of dollars constructing a barrier of steel and concrete between it and the rest of the Americas in an attempt to stymie the flow of illegal immigrants across the US-Mexican border. Diplomatically speaking, this is a slap in the face of every Latin American. Moreover, as evidenced by similar events throughout history (for example, the walls of Troy, 1200 BC; Berlin Wall, 1962; Gaza Strip, 1994; and West Bank walls in Israel, 2002), humans are intelligent enough to figure out ways around obstacles that stand between them and what they strongly desire. Unfortunately, the symbolic nature of the wall, separating the "rich Americans" from the "poor Americans," will only drive deeper the existing wedge between the two sides—further exasperating any attempt to reunite the Americas. This is exactly the type of diplomatic nightmare that is fueling the flames of leftism throughout the region, and it is what the United States needs to stop doing in order to increase its own national security.

One of the widely publicized reasons Latin American immigrants enter the United States is lack of opportunity to earn a decent living in their former country. Increasing job growth and redistributing wealth within the LAC region will help keep Latin Americans at home. Logic dictates that reducing the number of illegal immigrants attempting to enter the United States will make it easier for customs officials and border patrols to interdict shipments of illegal goods and defend against potential terrorist infiltration, thus making the United States more secure in the long run.

It appears as though the self-interest tactics displayed by the United States over the previous 50 years have allowed it to get its way during small points of contention but lose the big picture with regard to its own national security. Diplomatically and strategically, the United States is winning the battle but losing the war.

Notes

(All notes appear in shortened form. For full details, see the appropriate entry in the bibliography.)

1. Navarrette, "A Tall Order," 14.

2. For simplification, the scope of this research paper has been limited to these countries in the Caribbean, South America, and Central America, which are sovereign states and whose population exceeds one million: Argentina, Bolivia, Brazil, Chile, Colombia, Costa Rica, Cuba, Dominican Republic, Ecuador, El Salvador, Guatemala, Haiti, Honduras, Jamaica, Mexico, Nicaragua, Panama, Paraguay, Peru, Trinidad and Tobago, Uruguay, and Venezuela.

3. These are Argentina, Bolivia, Brazil, Chile, Cuba, Ecuador, Nicaragua, Peru, and Venezuela. MSNBC, "Leftward Tilt."

4. These include Albania, Bulgaria, Czechoslovakia, East Germany, Hungary, Poland, Romania, Soviet Union, and Yugoslavia.

5. US Agency for International Development, *U.S. Overseas Loans.*

6. Yassin, "Impact of Structural Adjustment Policies," 315.

7. Autocracies are not to be confused with populist governments of recent LAC fame whose presidential candidate promises to support the poorer citizens in their struggle against privileged elitists.

8. For the remainder of this paper the term "leftism" or "leftist" will be used to describe all forms of government that fall on the left side of this spectrum and result in a state-run economy.

9. Turner, *Statesman's Yearbook.*

10. His last term in office lasted only 11 days (1–11 October 1968).

11. Forero and Rohter, "Bolivia's Leader Solidifies."

12. Ferguson, "Want Historic Trouble?"

13. Examples include the French Revolution (1789) and the Russian Revolution (1917).

14. Oppenheimer, "Latin American Elites."

15. These countries are Australia, Austria, Belgium, Canada, Czech Republic, Denmark, Finland, France, Germany, Greece, Hungary, Iceland, Ireland, Italy, Japan, Korea, Luxembourg, Mexico, Netherlands, New Zealand, Norway, Poland, Portugal, Slovak Republic, Spain, Sweden, Switzerland, Turkey, United Kingdom, and United States.

16. Watkins, *Beyond Scarcity*, 334. The GDP-PPP for East Asia and the Pacific is $5,872; Arab States, $5,680; and South Asia, $3,072 (ibid.).

17. Ibid.

18. Yassin, "Impact of Structural Adjustment," 315.

19. De Ferranti et al., *Inequality in Latin America*, 416.

20. Ibid., 17.

21. Hurtado, *Social Dimension of Globalization*, 2.

22. De Ferranti et al., *Inequality in Latin America*, 407.

23. Lott, "Security Issues in Latin America."

24. Ter Horst, "Turning Left."

25. The Greenbook's official name is *The US Overseas Loans and Grants, Obligations and Loan Authorizations*; it documents US foreign aid.

26. USAID, *U.S. Overseas Loans and Grants*. The rise in US foreign aid to the LAC region following 1996 is due almost entirely to an increase in funding for the war on drugs (i.e., Plan Colombia).

27. Haugaard, *Tarnished Image*, 10.

28. "Of the 22 countries worldwide currently prohibited from receiving assistance, twelve are in Latin America and the Caribbean: Barbados, Bolivia, Brazil, Costa Rica, Ecuador, Mexico, Paraguay, Peru, St. Vincent and the Grenadines, Trinidad and Tobago, Uruguay and Venezuela" (ibid., 11).

29. Starr, "How the U.S. Went Wrong."

30. Haugaard, *Tarnished Image*, 12–13.

31. Aizenman, "Ortega Set to Reclaim."

32. Ferguson, "Want Historic Trouble?"

33. Countries with negative views of the United States are Argentina, 65 percent; Brazil, 51 percent; Chile, 50 percent; and Mexico, 57 percent. Those that view President Bush as a negative world influence are Argen-

tina, 79 percent; Brazil, 78 percent; Chile, 62 percent; and Mexico, 58 percent. Haugaard, *Tarnished Image*, 6.

34. Bachelet, "Bush Aide Seeks Better U.S. Image."

35. Oppenheimer, "Latin American Elites."

36. Bachelet, "Bush Aide Seeks Better U.S. Image."

37. Oppenheimer, "Latin American Elites."

38. Ibid.

39. De Ferranti et al., *Inequality in Latin America*, 421. Paraguay is a slight exception, dropping from 5.8 to 5.7 years; no data was available for Cuba.

40. Ibid. No adult literacy data was available for El Salvador, Haiti, Paraguay, Trinidad and Tobago, and Uruguay. No youth literacy data was available for these same countries, plus Jamaica.

41. Ibid.

42. Percentages in Nicaragua, Panama, and Uruguay declined. No data was available for the remaining eight countries. Watkins, *Beyond Scarcity*, 323–26.

43. Bush, *National Security Strategy*, cover letter.

44. Bush, *National Strategy for Combating Terrorism*, 3.

45. The recent election of Hamas as head of the Palestinian Authority is another example.

46. Ferguson, "Want Historic Trouble?"

47. Salazar, "Cuba's Foreign Policy."

48. Monreal, "Cuban Development."

49. Crespo, "Other 'Axis of Evil.' "

50. Emerson, "Blood Money."

51. Crespo, "Other 'Axis of Evil.' "

52. Robinson, "Terror Close to Home."

53. Ibid.

54. Crespo, "Venezuela."

55. Bennett and Webster, "Inside the Revolutionary Armed Forces."

56. Crespo, "Venezuela."

57. Ibid.

58. Crespo, "Other 'Axis of Evil.' "

59. Emerson, "Blood Money."

60. Crespo, "Other 'Axis of Evil.' "

61. Ibid.

62. Ibid.

63. Ibid.

64. Carl, "Iran Leader Courts Latin America Allies."

65. Ibid.

66. Forero and Rohter, "Bolivia's Leader Solidifies."

67. Kenny, "China's Presence in Latin America," 61. Adm Alejandro Kenny, Argentine navy, retired, is the former commandant of the Argentine Southern Naval Zone at Ushuaia, Tierra del Fuego, and is currently serving as an advisor on policy and strategy to the Argentine naval and combined general staffs.

68. Chinese trade is up 36 percent with Cuba in 2004, up 44 percent with Mexico in 2004, up 69 percent with Brazil in 2003 (China's number-one trading partner), and up 50 percent with Chile in 2004 (the

first Latin American country to sign a free-trade agreement with the PRC). Ibid., 61–62.

69. Kenny, "China's Presence in Latin America," 61.

70. Ibid., 64, 66.

71. Starr, "How the U.S. Went Wrong."

72. Forero, "Opposition to U.S."

73. Reuters, "Chavez Poses Threat."

74. Carl, "Latin American Leftists."

75. Oppenheimer, "In Latin America."

76. Forero, "Seeking United Latin America."

77. Ferguson, "Want Historic Trouble?"

78. Brazil is the "world's second-largest cocaine-consuming country." Oppenheimer, "In Latin America."

79. Forero and Rohter, "Bolivia's Leader Solidifies."

80. Ibid.

81. Ibid.

82. Sabatini and Farnsworth, "Latin America's Lurch."

83. Ibid.

84. Forero, "Elections Could Tilt."

85. Ter Horst, "Turning Left?"

86. Contreras, "Call of the Radical Center."

87. Oppenheimer, "Vote on Peru Trade Deal."

88. Forero, "Elections Could Tilt."

89. Oppenheimer, "In Latin America."

90. Friedman, *Lexus and the Olive Tree*, 248–75. Friedman observes that "Argentina didn't get its first McDonald's until 1986, four years after" it fought the Falklands War against Great Britain (ibid., 249).

91. Ibid., 248–75.

92. Haugaard, *Tarnished Image*, 15.

93. Oppenheimer, "Chávez Making Friends."

Bibliography

Aizenman, Nurith Celina. "Ortega Set to Reclaim Nicaraguan Presidency." *Washington Post* Foreign Service, 7 November 2006.

Bachelet, Pablo. "Bush Aide Seeks Better U.S. Image in Latin America." *Miami Herald*, 18 April 2006.

Bennett, Jerris L., and Kelly L. Webster. "Inside the Revolutionary Armed Forces of Colombia (FARC)." *Kennedy School Review* 4 (2003): 35–51.

Bush, George W. *The National Security Strategy of the United States of America*. Washington, DC: The White House, 2006.

———. *National Strategy for Combating Terrorism*. Washington, DC: Executive Office of the President, 2003.

Carl, Traci. "Iran Leader Courts Latin America Allies." Associated Press, 14 January 2007.

———. "Latin American Leftists Redefine Politics." Associated Press, 20 March 2006.

Contreras, Joseph. "The Call of the Radical Center: Daniel Ortega; All Signs Suggest the Chastened Sandinista Firebrand Will Embrace Moderation This Time Around." *Newsweek* (international edition), 25 December 2006.

Crespo, Paul. "The Other 'Axis of Evil.' " *American Legion Magazine*, 1 July 2003.

———. "Venezuela: The Next Cuba." *FrontPage Magazine*, 3 March 2004. http://www.frontpagemag.com/Articles/Read.aspx?GUID=7DF65966-CF48-4786-A651-67B006CEE6CB.

De Ferranti, David, Guillermo Perry, Francisco H. G. Ferreira, and Michael Walton. *Inequality in Latin America and the Caribbean: Breaking with History?* Washington, DC: World Bank, 2004.

Emerson, Steven. "Blood Money: Hezbollah's Revenue Stream Flows through the Americas." *American Legion Magazine*, March 2007.

Ferguson, Niall. "Want Historic Trouble? Look South." *Los Angeles Times*, 13 February 2006.

Forero, Juan. "Elections Could Tilt Latin America Further to the Left." *New York Times*, 10 December 2005.

———. "Opposition to U.S. Makes Chavez a Hero to Many." *New York Times*, 2 June 2005 (corrected copy).

———. "Seeking United Latin America, Venezuela's Chavez is a Divider." *New York Times*, 20 May 2006.

Forero, Juan, and Larry Rohter. "Bolivia's Leader Solidifies Region's Leftward Tilt." *New York Times*, 22 January 2006.

Friedman, Thomas. *The Lexus and the Olive Tree.* New York: Random House (Paperback), 2000.

Haugaard, Lisa. *Tarnished Image: Latin America Perceives the United States.* Washington, DC: Latin America Working Group, March 2006. http://www.lawg.org/docs/tarnishedimage.pdf.

Hurtado, Alvaro Garcia. *The Social Dimension of Globalization in Latin America: Lessons from Bolivia and Chile.* Working Paper no. 23. Geneva: International Labour Office, May 2004.

Kenny, Alejandro. "China's Presence in Latin America: A View on Security from the Southern Cone." *Military Review* (September–October 2006): 60–66.

Lott, Anthony D. "Security Issues in Latin America." Lecture. Air Command and Staff College, Montgomery, AL, 30 October 2006. (Permission to cite lecture material provided by Dr. Anthony Lott via e-mail to the author, 7 March 2007.)

Monreal, Pedro. "Cuban Development in the Bolivarian Matrix." *NACLA Report on the Americas* 39, no. 4 (January–February 2006): 22–27.

MSNBC. "Leftward Tilt: Political Shift in Latin America." http://www.msnbc.msn.com/id/10927120.

Navarrette, Ruben, Jr. "A Tall Order for Mexico's President-Elect." *Hispanic* 19, no. 9 (September 2006): 14–15.

Oppenheimer, Andres. "Chávez Making Friends While Bush Earning Enmity." *Miami Herald*, 9 February 2006.

———. "In Latin America, It's the Left vs. the Left." *Miami Herald*, 7 May 2006.

———. "Latin American Elites No Big Fans of U.S." *Miami Herald*, 25 September 2005.

———. "Vote on Peru Trade Deal May Be Now or Never." *Miami Herald*, 13 July 2006.

Reuters. "Chavez Poses Threat to Democracy: Negroponte," 30 January 2007. http://www.reuters.com/article/politicsNews/idUSN3037023720070130.

Robinson, Linda. "Terror Close to Home in Oil-Rich Venezuela: A Volatile Leader Befriends Bad Actors from the Mideast, Colombia, and Cuba." *U.S. News and World Report* 135, no. 11 (6 October 2003): 20.

Sabatini, Christopher A., and Eric Farnsworth. "Latin America's Lurch to the Left." *Christian Science Monitor*, 13 February 2006. http://www.csmonitor.com/2006/0213/p09s02-coop.html.

Salazar, Luis Suárez. "Cuba's Foreign Policy and the Promise of ALBA." *NACLA Report on the Americas* 39, no. 4 (January–February 2006): 27–32.

Starr, Alexandra. "How the U.S. Went Wrong in Latin America." *Christian Science Monitor*, 15 March 2006.

Ter Horst, Enrique. "Turning Left, but Down Which Road?" *International Herald Tribune*, 18 January 2006.

Turner, Barry, ed. *The Statesman's Yearbook 2007: The Politics, Cultures and Economies of the World.* 143rd ed. New York: Palgrave Macmillan, 2006.

US Agency for International Development. *U.S. Overseas Loans and Grants: Obligations and Loan Authorizations, July 1, 1945–September 30, 2006* ("The Greenbook"). http://qesdb.cdie.org/gbk/index.html.

Watkins, Kevin. *Beyond Scarcity: Power, Poverty and the Global Water Crisis.* Human Development Report 2006. New York: United Nations Development Programme, 2006.

Yassin, Khaled M. "Impact of Structural Adjustment Policies on Health in Developing Countries." Doctoral thesis, Bielefeld University (Germany), January 2002.

www.ingramcontent.com/pod-product-compliance
Lightning Source LLC
Chambersburg PA
CBHW060017300526
45794CB00003B/1207